W9-BVH-685

# Full Access TO MUSIC'S BEST AND BRIGHTEST

# BACKSTAGE PASS

## Mary Boone

TRIUMPH
BOOKS

Copyright © 2013 by Triumph Books LLC

No part of this publication may be reproduced, stored in a retrieval system, or transmitted in any form by any means, electronic, mechanical, photocopying, or otherwise, without the prior written permission of the publisher, Triumph Books LLC, 814 North Franklin Street, Chicago, Illinois 60610.

This book is available in quantity at special discounts for your group or organization. For further information, contact:

Triumph Books LLC
814 North Franklin Street
Chicago, Illinois 60610
Phone: (312) 337-0747
www.triumphbooks.com

Printed in U.S.A.

ISBN: 978-1-60078-977-9

Content developed and packaged by Rockett Media, Inc.
Writer: Mary Boone
Editor: Bob Baker
Design: Andrew Burwell
Page production: Chad Bell
Cover design by Andrew Burwell

Photographs courtesy of Getty Images unless otherwise noted

This book is not authorized, approved, or endorsed by the entertainers included herein or any organization or entity associated with or affiliated with these entertainers. It is not an official publication.

# Full Access TO MUSIC'S BEST AND BRIGHTEST
# BACKSTAGE PASS

**W**orldwide, the music industry generated more than $67.6 billion in revenue in 2011 – that's more than the combined national expenditures of the governments of Ecuador, Libya and Lithuania.

Why are we spending so much cash on CDs, digital downloads and concert tickets?

Because music touches us like few other things can. Whether you prefer rap or pop or country, you're sure to have songs that "speak" to you. Some of those special melodies will stay with you throughout your life: the song that was playing when you had your first kiss, the song that played over and over during a favorite spring break trip, the song that was played at your grandmother's funeral. Sometimes lyrics can say what we can't. And sometimes the lyrics are secondary to a raucous guitar riff or ferocious drum solo.

In these pages, we profile 10 of the hottest musicians in the world today. Collectively, these artists have sold hundreds of millions of albums, earned 29 Grammy nominations, received 131 Teen Choice Award nominations, and amassed more than 247.8 million Twitter followers.

Here's to the artists who sing the soundtracks of our lives…

Singer Bruno Mars performs the 2011 MTV Europe Awards in Belfast. Bruno has earned eight MTV Europe nominations and two awards.

Taylor Swift and Ed Sheeran hang out prior to performing on Taylor's RED Tour. The North American leg of the tour lasted six months and played to a combined audience of 1.2 million people.

# CHAPTER ONE

## Selena Gomez

Selena Gomez is about to take a break from music. Or not. It depends on which day you ask her. While promoting her movie *Getaway*, Selena told the media she was putting her recording career on hold in order to focus on acting. Maybe.

"I'm a woman so I change my mind all the time," she said during an August 2013 news conference. "One day I want to do acting and just that, and then other times I just want to do music and just that, so it changes."

It's likely two major factors will help Selena decide where to direct her energies, at least in the short term:

- Her 2013 Stars Dance World Tour has been warmly received, with critics calling it "an inspirational experience" and "classy celebration."
- *Getaway* has been universally panned. *Rolling Stone's* Peter Travers wrote: "The damage to your brain while watching it is incalculable." And Bilge Ebiri of *Vulture* called it "the dumbest movie released this summer."

Fans, of course, hope Selena will continue to balance acting and music – and fashion

# ALL ACCESS

| | |
|---|---|
| **Full name:** | Selena Marie Gomez |
| **Genre:** | Pop |
| **First big hit:** | "Come & Get It," the lead track from Selena's album **Stars Dance**, climbed to No. 6 on the Billboard Hot 100 (her first top 10) and No. 2 on the Pop Songs airplay chart. |
| **Label:** | Hollywood Records |
| **Website:** | www.selenagomez.com |
| **On Twitter:** | @selenagomez |
| **Twitter followers:** | 16.8 million |
| **Reputation:** | Selena has remade herself over and over again. From a kid actress on *Barney & Friends* to Disney stardom in *Wizards of Waverly Place* to dating Justin Bieber – she's morphed into a respected musician. |
| **Why we love her:** | Loads of child stars have sneaked their way into jobs as teens or young adults. There was no sneaking for Selena. She's the real deal: talented, beautiful, driven, strategic – and appreciative of the fans who adore her. |

and philanthropy and whatever else she can fit into her schedule.

Selena Marie Gomez was born July 22, 1992, to Amanda "Mandy" Cornett Teefey and Ricardo Gomez; her mother was just 16 when she was born. Selena's parents split up when she was young and she was primarily raised by her mother, who struggled financially.

"I remember my mom would run out of gas all of the time; we'd sit there and have to go through the car and get quarters to help her buy gas, because she never liked to ask my grandparents for money," Selena told *E! Entertainment* in 2011. "My mom gave up everything for me, had three jobs, supported me, sacrificed her life for me."

Selena, who grew up in Grand Prairie, Texas, was inspired to try her hand at acting after watching her mother perform in local theater.

Selena launched her career at age 7 when she won a role on the TV series *Barney & Friends*. Commercials and small roles followed. When she was 11, a poncho-wearing Selena first auditioned for the Disney Channel; she won small parts on *The Suite Life of Zack and Cody* and *Hannah Montana*.

A year later, Selena's life changed when she was cast as Alex Russo in *Wizards of Waverly Place*. The Emmy Award-winning show made Selena one of the most recognized teens on the planet.

The big screen was a logical next step. Selena earned her first major role as Beezus in 2010's *Ramona and Beezus*. A year later, she starred in *Monte Carlo*. Edgier movie roles followed; Selena starred with Ashley

Benson and Vanessa Hudgens in 2012's *Spring Breakers* and she worked with Ethan Hawke and Jon Voight in 2013's *Getaway*.

The young actress has lead roles in two movies slated for release in 2014: She stars alongside Natt Wolff, Elizabeth Shue and Mary-Louise Parker in *Behaving Badly* and in William H. Macy's dark drama *Rudderless*.

Selena first got a chance to showcase her singing skills on the *Wizards of Waverly Place* soundtrack. In 2008, she signed a deal with Hollywood Records. She released her first three albums – *Kiss and Tell, A Year Without Rain* and *When the Sun Goes Down* – with her band, Selena Gomez & the Scene.

In July 2013, Selena, released her first solo album, *Stars Dance*. In its first week, the album sold 97,000 copies and bumped Jay Z from the top spot on the Billboard 200.

While fans clearly love *Stars Dance*, the project received mixed reviews:

*"Stars Dance" is exactly the kind of album one makes in 2013 if you want to keep the pop sugar of the Disney tween cabal but mix in some broken glass and a club bathroom nosebleed."*
– *Los Angeles Times*

*"Fans of dance music, particularly Europop, will find plenty to enjoy here."*
– *The New Zealand Herald*

*"If she really wants to be considered a grown-up pop star, Selena*

*Gomez is going to have to find some better hit-makers."*
*– The (London) Guardian*

As tough as her critics may be, Selena is even tougher on herself. She admits she's struggled with growing up in the spotlight. She knows her audience is still primarily teens and tweens, so she strives to keep her shows classy; she doesn't dangle her tongue or twerk. Still, her lyrics are laced with R-rated innuendo.

"I think I'm still making the transition from kid Selena into adult," she told Entertainmentwise.com in 2013. "It's not an easy transition and I don't think I've crossed the path yet. I've still got a lot of proving myself to do."

When she's not making music or movies, Selena is proving herself to be a savvy businesswoman. She's been the brand ambassador for the adidas NEO Label since 2012 and launched her first clothing line for teens through adidas in 2013.

In 2009, the songstress became the Unit-ed States' youngest UNICEF Ambassador. On her first UNICEF field mission, Selena traveled to Ghana, where she worked with teams providing essentials including clean water, food and medicine.

Even more than her music, movies or charitable efforts, it's Selena's personal life that's been the subject of headlines: feuds with pals Demi Lovato and Taylor Swift, disses by newcomer Lorde and, of course, links to any guy with whom she's photographed. Her on again-off again relationship with Justin Bieber has been the subject of articles in publications ranging from People to the *Wall Street Journal*.

"It does get to me. I'm a human and I feel those emotions when people talk about you," she told the *New York Daily News* in 2013. "It's never a good feeling 'cause half the time it's just bull, it's not real."

What is real is this: Whether it's in music or TV or movies, it's likely Selena Gomez is going to be a force to be reckoned with for many years to come.

Selena Gomez performs in Louisville, Kentucky, in October 2013 as part of her Stars Dance Tour.

Selena Gomez arrives at the California premiere of her movie *Getaway* in August 2013.

# CHAPTER TWO

Ariana Grande

Sure, she's a veteran of Broadway and television, but it's the musical world that Florida native Ariana Grande has been hoping to conquer. And now, it appears, she has.

Already famous for her roles on Nickelodeon's *Victorious* and *Sam & Cat*, Ariana's debut album, *Yours Truly*, was released September 3, 2013, and went straight to the top of the Billboard 200 chart.

The young pop singer had already been hailed as the "new Mariah Carey" and now she is proving herself. According to Billboard, she is one of just 15 solo female artists whose debut albums have opened at No. 1.

Ariana became interested in theater as a child, starting with small parts in community theater productions. As her experience grew, so did the size of the roles she won and the venues in which she performed. In 2008, she won a National Youth Theatre Association Award for her portrayal of a cheerleader named Charlotte in the Broadway production of *13*.

In 2009, Ariana began performing at New York City jazz clubs. Then, in 2010, her career really took off. She played the role of Miriam in the first reading of *Cuba Libre*, a

## ALL ACCESS

| | |
|---|---|
| **Full name:** | Ariana Grande-Butera |
| **Genre:** | R&B, pop and soul |
| **First big hit:** | "The Way," featuring rapper Mac Miller, was released on iTunes on March 26, 2013; within seven hours of its release, it was at No. 1 on iTunes' Top Singles chart. The song also debuted on the Billboard Hot 100 at No. 10. |
| **Label:** | Republic |
| **Website:** | www.arianagrande.com |
| **On Twitter:** | @arianagrande |
| **Twitter followers:** | 10.4 million |
| **Reputation:** | Ariana got her start as an actress, performing in the show *13* on Broadway in 2008. She became widely known for her portrayal of the character Cat Valentine on the Nickelodeon sitcom *Victorious*. |
| **Why we love her:** | She's a multi-talented performer, generous philanthropist, and has taken a lead role in Hollywood's battle against bullying. What's not to love? |

musical composed by songwriter Desmond Child. And, when Nickelodeon put out a casting call for its new show, *Victorious*, Ariana was selected over hundreds of hopefuls who showed up.

"You know, you go into auditions and say, 'Hopefully they like me,'" she told the (Fla.) *Sun Sentinel* in 2010. "The original audition was (where) everybody had the same character, boy or girl, and you had to read the lines and act a little crazy. They called me back and asked me to try for Cat."

In addition to landing the role of Caterina Valentine, Ariana got a new hair color to go with it. Cat is a bubbly high schooler whose hair is the color of a red velvet cupcake.

"That was (producer) Dan Schneider's vision for my character," said the natural brunette. "It was totally genius and I can't see my character any other way ... When I dyed my hair it gave me a new energy that I could bring into the character."

Ariana gave life to Cat Valentine through 2013, the whole time taking on side projects as her schedule allowed. For instance, she provided the voice for Princess Diaspro on the Nick series *Winx Club* and starred as Snow White alongside Charlene Tilton and Neil Patrick Harris in a Pasadena Playhouse production of *A Snow White Christmas*.

Ariana's *Victorious* series ended in February 2013 –the same time her singing career took off. Her breakout single for Republic Records, "The Way" featuring Mac Miller, was released March 26, 2013. Seven hours after its release on the iTunes Store, "The Way" topped its Top Singles chart. It went Platinum in just 10 weeks and scored Ariana

her first Billboard Top 10. "The Way" was the first single released from *Yours Truly*, an album steeped in R&B.

With her music career humming along, Ariana signed onto another TV project. In Nickelodeon's *Sam & Cat*, which premiered in June 2013, Ariana's character, Cat, meets Jennette McCurdy's *iCarly* character Sam. The show focuses on the roommates as they start a babysitting business. The show has been Nick's No. 1 live-action series, but critics wonder how long Ariana can balance TV and music?

"It's hard to manage the two," she told *ET* in September 2013. "I'm doing two full-time jobs at once. But it's important to me. I really love doing *Sam & Cat*. I'm not ready to give up playing Cat Valentine ... I love my music as well, so I just want to make it work. It's much more work than anybody could ever imagine, but it's definitely worth it because I'm getting to do what I love."

The work may be difficult and the hours may be long, but it's clear Ariana's efforts are paying off. *Yours Truly* has been well received:

> *Ariana Grande's debut LP is a surprisingly varied affair for a 20-year-old Nickelodeon star with a devastatingly strong voice.*
> – *Billboard magazine*

> *This might be the most inviting pop record of 2013, with a bubbly ebullience that makes even its most familiar moves feel fresh.*
> – *Los Angeles Times*

*Yours Truly is a brilliant debut album from a singer who has gargantuan potential. The material is well written and produced and Grande performs each and every song with passion and nuance.*
— *StarPulse.com*

Even songstress Katy Perry has sung Ariana's praises.

"I love her," Perry told Sirius XM. "I think she has the best female vocal in pop music today. She has literally the best voice, the best voice live. She kills it. She's so good."

Those are the sorts of commendations that could cause a pop star's ego to inflate. But not Ariana. She's too busy planning her next step.

If things go according to Ariana's plan, her singing may soon take place on an even larger scale – as in a worldwide tour. "I want to get overseas and meet everybody over there and perform for them," she told *Billboard* magazine in October 2013. "I think that'd be a great experience." The young soprano already had her first headlining tour, a month-long outing called The Listening Sessions. She joined Justin Bieber as an opening act on his Believe tour for three shows in August 2013. She's also hard at work on her second album, tentatively scheduled for a February 2014 release.

For a girl who grew up writing songs in her room on GarageBand, having an album and getting radio play is a dream come true. And it's one Ariana hopes continues for a long time.

"I want to take it one day at a time obviously," she told *Elle* in October 2013. "I want to be a recording artist for my whole, entire life."

Ariana Grande performs at the 10th annual Style Awards during Mercedes-Benz Fashion Week in September 2013.

Ariana Grande
arrives at the 2013
Radio Disney Music
Awards at Nokia
Theatre L.A. Live on
April 27, 2013.

# CHAPTER THREE

# Taylor Swift

Taylor Swift isn't afraid of music critics, snarky producers or even rude rap stars (think Kanye West). That's not to say she doesn't have her share of anxiety.

"I'm intimidated by the fear of being average," she admitted during a 2006 interview.

Average?

When searching for words to describe Taylor, "average" hardly ever comes into play. Writers have called her "beautiful," "gifted" and "genuine" – but never average.

Average kids don't start writing songs while they're still in kindergarten. They don't, at age 11, show up at record companies announcing they want to record an album. And then, when they get a deal at age 13, they certainly don't back out of their contract because they don't want to sing other writers' songs.

Taylor Alison Swift is a lot of things, but average isn't one of them.

Taylor grew up in southeastern Pennsylvania and got her love of music from her grandmother, Marjorie Finlay, an opera singer.

Her parents regularly made the two-and-a-half-hour trip from their home to New York City to attend Broadway performances and for singing and acting lessons. While still in elementary school, Taylor fell in love with musical theater. After a few years of auditions and not getting any roles, she turned her attention

## ALL ACCESS

| | |
|---|---|
| **Full name:** | Taylor Alison Swift |
| **Genre:** | Country, country pop, country rock |
| **First big hit:** | "Tim McGraw," the first single from her debut self-titled album, broke the Top Ten on Billboard Music's Country Charts. |
| **Label:** | Big Machine |
| **Website:** | www.taylorswift.com |
| **On Twitter:** | @taylorswift13 |
| **Twitter followers:** | 35.4 million |
| **Reputation:** | If you break Taylor's heart, she's probably going to write a song about you – just ask John Mayer, Joe Jonas, Taylor Lautner or Harry Styles. |
| **Why we love her:** | If you take away the sequins and glitz, she really is a normal twenty-something. No pretenses, no fights with the paparazzi; just a girl who can sing. |

SWAROVSKI
ENTERTAINMENT

ROMEO & JULIET

SWAROVSKI
ENTERTAINMENT

to country music.

When she was 11, Taylor won a talent competition. As a prize, she got to appear as the opening act at a show being performed by singer Charlie Daniels. For Taylor, this was a step toward achieving her dreams but it was just a small step. She was certain she could find true success if she could just get to Nashville.

And so, she went.

"I took my demo CDs of karaoke songs, where I sound like a chipmunk – it's pretty awesome – to Nashville, and my mom waited in the car while I knocked on doors up and down Music Row," she told *Entertainment Weekly* in 2008. "I would say, 'Hi, I'm Taylor. I'm 11. I want a record deal. Call me.'"

She received rejections along the way, but instead of giving up, she learned to play the guitar and began to focus on songwriting. Her supportive family relocated to the Nashville suburb of Hendersonville.

In 2004, at age 14, Taylor began working with a talent agency. A year later, her family dropped the agent but not before meeting with some of Nashville's major record labels. After performing at a RCA Records showcase, she got a development deal.

Taylor had been working for years to get a record deal, so it was a difficult decision for the teen to nix the contract when RCA insisted she sing other writer's songs. Around that same time, she became the youngest songwriter to sign a publishing deal with Sony – with the stipulation that she didn't want her songs sung by other artists. She was young but she knew what she wanted.

Music industry veteran Scott Borchetta met Taylor shortly after her RCA deal fell apart. He was planning a new label, Big Machine Records, and was thrilled to sign Taylor.

Her self-titled debut was released when she was 16 years old. She wrote all 11 songs on the album. "Our Song," her third single, became a gigantic hit and made her the youngest person ever to both write and perform a No. 1 song on the country charts. She received a Best New Artist nomination at the 2008 Grammy Awards.

As with her debut, Swift wrote or co-wrote all 13 tracks on her second album, *Fearless*. The CD topped the Billboard 200 for 11 weeks and became the biggest selling record of 2009. *Fearless* earned Taylor four Grammy Awards: Album of the Year, Best Country Album, Best Country Song (for "White Horse") and Best Female Country Vocal Performance.

Taylor's third album, 2010's *Speak Now*, sold more than 1 million copies in its first week of release in the United States. The album yielded two No. 1 country hits – "Sparks Fly" and "Ours." Another single, "Mean," won Grammy Awards for Best Country Song and Best Country Solo Performance.

Taylor's latest album, *Red*, was released Oct. 22, 2012. *Red* sold 1.2 million copies in its first week – the largest sales week for any album in a decade. It was Taylor's second straight album to sell more than 1 million copies in its first week. According to Nielsen SoundScan, she's the only female artist to have two albums sell more than 1 million copies during their debut weeks.

When it came time to tally up the best-selling albums of 2012, *Red* came in at No. 2, just behind Adele's *21*. It was the fourth time Taylor had an album in the year-end top three.

Part of *Red*'s appeal may be the passion with which it was created.

"I made the emotion of the song a priority rather than asking, 'What should we do from a production standpoint, or what works in this genre?'" Taylor told *Billboard* magazine prior to the album's release. "Instead, it was, 'What did that emotion feel like when I wrote the song?' And whatever the answer was, it determined what the track sounded like and what my vocals were supposed to sound like."

In March 2013, Taylor began the 66-show North American leg of her *Red* concert tour. According to Pollstar, from January to June 2013, Red was the second-highest grossing North American tour; Taylor did 37 shows in 27 cities during the first half of the year, with $58.5 million in earnings. Only the Rolling Stones, with an average ticket price of $346.09, ranked higher; that band's 18 early 2013 shows grossed

$87.7 million.

In October 2013, Taylor stopped by Nashville's Country Music Hall of Fame and Museum, to celebrate the opening of the $4 million education center she donated to the museum as part of its expansion campaign. The Taylor Swift Education Center includes classrooms and a children's area filled with interactive exhibits. Taylor's even been working with staff to figure out how she can participate in educational programs at the center.

"We've been talking about different programs I can be involved in," she told the Associated Press. "I hate to call it a lecture because that sounds like I'm yelling at people, but we could do a Q&A talking to students here and a songwriters discussion would be really fun to have at some point."

Talented singer, insightful songwriter, savvy businesswoman, caring music mentor – it's all in a day's work for anything-but-average Taylor Swift.

Taylor Swift performs during Tim McGraw's 2013 Superstar Summer Night at the MGM Grand Garden Arena in Las Vegas.

# CHAPTER FOUR

## Demi Lovato

Excitement. That's what Demi Lovato wanted from her fourth studio album. She wanted songs on the album to excite her and she wanted its lyrics and pop and dance-stylings to excite fans.

Her plan worked. When *Demi* was released by Hollywood Records in May 2013, it charted at No. 3 on the U.S. Billboard 200 with first-week sales of 110,000 copies. It became the best-selling debut of her career. The album was similarly successful in international markets; it reached the Top 5 in Canada, Mexico and Spain and it became her first album to chart in the United Kingdom, at No. 3.

The album's lead single, "Heart Attack," became Demi's third highest-charting U.S. single when it peaked at No. 10 on the Billboard Hot 100.

One of Demi's new motivating factors is that she's decided she really wants her music to be a beacon of positivity.

"I always want to make positive music," she told *PopCrush* in May 2013. It's true, Demi has evolved these past few years, both personally and professionally.

Born August 20, 1992, in Albuquerque, New Mexico, Demi is the middle of three children; her parents split up when she was just a baby. Her mom, Dianna De La Garza,

# ALL ACCESS

| | |
|---|---|
| **Full name:** | Demetria Devonne Lovato |
| **Genre:** | Pop, rock and R&B |
| **First big hit:** | "Here We Go Again," the lead single from Demi's second studio album, peaked at No. 15 on the Billboard Hot 100 and became her first top 40 hit as a solo artist. |
| **Label:** | Hollywood Records |
| **Website:** | www.demilovato.com |
| **On Twitter:** | @ddlovato |
| **Twitter followers:** | 19 million |
| **Reputation:** | Demi got her start as a child actress on *Barney & Friends* and made a successful transition to a serious music career. She's respected throughout the industry for her toughness. |
| **Why we love her:** | Flat out, the girl can sing! |

Demi Lovato performs at the 2013 Teen Choice Awards in Universal City, California. Since 2009, Demi has earned 24 Teen Choice nominations and she's won 10 of the coveted surfboard awards.

was a former Dallas Cowboys cheerleader and country singer who passed her love of entertaining onto her children (Demi's sisters Dallas Lovato and Madison De La Garza are both singers/actresses).

As a young child, Demi entered – and won – her share of beauty pageants and talent competitions. She earned the right to perform in some pretty prestigious venues including the 2002 Dallas Cowboys' Thanksgiving Day Halftime Show with country singer LeAnn Rimes.

At age 10, Demi officially launched her career by earning a regular role on the children's TV series *Barney & Friends*. Guest spots in other shows followed and, in 2007, Demi landed the role of Charlotte Adams on the Disney Channel comedy *As the Bell Rings*.

She left that show after just one season because she got an even bigger role: Demi was cast as Mitchie Torres in the 2008 Disney Channel movie *Camp Rock*.

Not only did she star in the movie, but she also recorded three songs with The Jonas Brothers for the film's soundtrack. Demi was officially a "star."

In September 2008, she released her debut album, *Don't Forget*. The album debuted at No. 2 on the Billboard 200 chart and earned her a spot as the opening act on the Jonas Brothers' Burning Up Tour.

In 2009, Demi landed the role of Sonny Munroe in the Disney series *Sonny with a Chance* and released her second studio album, *Here We Go Again*.

The success was amazing but the stress was overwhelming.

In late 2010, Demi was admitted to Timberline Knolls, a rehab center in Illinois.

Recovery was difficult but, with the support of family, friends, and fans, Demi persevered. When she was released from treatment in early 2011, she quit *Sonny with a Chance* and focused her attention on music.

Demi's third studio album, *Unbroken*, was released in September 2011. The album peaked at No. 4 on the U.S. Billboard 200 and yielded two Top 20 singles: "Skyscraper" and "This is Me."

As much as fans adored *Unbroken*, Demi says it wasn't a true representation of herself.

"I got sick of the songs," she told *PopCrush*. "When I would play them onstage, I was just like, 'Oh my gosh, I can't play these anymore.' And I have to wonder, was that album really who I was? Was I just experimenting with sounds? I think I wanted to try something more R&B, but when I tried that, it wasn't really me."

Demi wrote 10 of the 13 songs on her newest album and recorded it while serving as a judge on the American version of *The X Factor*. She's announced a 2014 tour featuring Little Mix, Cher Lloyd and Fifth Harmony.

As well-received as Demi's new music has been, she says recording and touring are not part of her long-term plan.

"I think I'm going to work really, really hard for the next couple years and then after that, just settle down and either have a family, or travel the world and do just a bunch of charity stuff and just spend time with my family," she told *Parade* in March 2013.

A music scene without Demi? That's tough for fans to imagine. Until that day comes, they'll keep humming along to "positive" music from an artist they positively adore.

Demi Lovato performs a May 2013 show in London as part of the "VEVO Presents Live" series.

Demi Lovato arrives on the red carpet at the 2013 MuchMusic Video Awards in Toronto, Canada.

# CHAPTER FIVE

# Carly Rae Jepsen

As the artist behind 2012's most infectious song, Carly Rae Jepsen skyrocketed to worldwide fame. "Call Me Maybe" has inspired lip dub tributes by nursing home residents, Olympic swimmers, U.S. Army troops, bridal parties and more. The song has been covered by everyone from fellow musicians (Katy Perry, Justin Bieber) to talk-show hosts (Jimmy Fallon, Gayle King) to politicians (former Australian Prime Minister Kevin Rudd, former U.S. Secretary of State Colin Powell).

Carly Rae, who already had two gold singles, a full-length album and EP, and two Juno Award nominations in her home country of Canada, was virtually unknown in the States. Then, with a little help from fellow Canadian Justin Bieber, she hit it big – really big.

Bieber told *NBC's Rock Center with Brian Williams* he was in Canada in late 2011 when he first heard the single on the radio.

"I was just like, 'This is probably the

# ALL ACCESS

| | |
|---|---|
| **Full name:** | Carly Rae Jepsen |
| **Genre:** | Pop, rock and folk |
| **First big hit:** | Carly Rae's single "Call Me Maybe" had the world singing along when it was released in September 2011. The song was the best-selling single worldwide in 2012, selling more than 10 million copies in that year alone. |
| **Label:** | School Boy Records |
| **Website:** | www.carlyraemusic.com |
| **On Twitter:** | @carlyraejepsen |
| **Twitter followers:** | 9 million |
| **Reputation:** | When Carly Rae first hit the scene, she was known "as the singer Justin Bieber discovered." It's true, JB got her signed to his label and used his social media connections to spread the word about her, but Carly Rae has stayed in the spotlight thanks to some real musical talent. |
| **Why we love her:** | "Call Me Maybe" put her on the map, but Carly Rae isn't content to rest on her laurels. This girl has been recording and touring like crazy. Plus, she's cute as a button. |

Carly Rae Jepsen made headlines when she threw out the first pitch at a 2013 MLB game between the Tampa Bay Rays and the Houston Astros. It's a good thing she can sing because her pitch bounced just a few feet from the pitcher's mound.

catchiest song I've ever heard in my whole life.' Like, 'Who thought of this song?'" he said. "All my friends in the car, 18-year-old guys, are singing this song and I'm like, 'Who is this person?'"

Bieber tweeted about the song to his millions of followers and teamed up with Selena Gomez, Ashley Tisdale and others to create a now-viral video for the song. As if that wasn't enough, he ultimately signed Carly Rae to Schoolboy Records, the label he runs with his manager Scooter Braun.

Carly Rae says it's only natural that Bieber's name comes up whenever she does a media interview.

"I never get tired of being asked about him," she told *Cosmopolitan* magazine in January 2012. "I'm forever indebted to him for the lovely boost that he's given me."

As grateful as she is for the success of "Call Me Maybe" (it has sales of more than 13 million, received two Grammy nominations and was named 2012 Song of the Year by MTV), Carly Rae is glad to be able to show the world she's not a one-hit wonder.

"I think if I had felt like 'Call Me Maybe' wasn't a good representation of who I am as an artist, it would have been very daunting," she told the *Los Angeles Times* in February 2013. "Luckily it's right in the lane of the avenue of the type of music that I love. It is lighthearted and optimistic and slightly flirtatious.  It's a song that today, after singing it countless times, I'm still having a ball with it because it doesn't feel like mine anymore. It feels like the whole world gets to sing it with me and it's a celebration."

She says she considers the song a "step-ping stone."

"I'm looking forward to showing that I've got other sides to me as well, and getting the platform to showcase those sides," she said.

The singer-songwriter from Mission, British Columbia, released her second studio album, *Kiss*, in September 2012. After her debut, *Tug of War*, which was successful in Canada but was never released worldwide, *Kiss* became Carly Rae's first internationally released album.

The album debuted at No. 6 on the Billboard 200, selling more than 46,000 copies in its opening week. Two singles, "Call Me Maybe" and "Good Time" – a duet with electronica musician Owl City – were released before the album's debut. After the album dropped, two more singles were released: "The Kiss" in September 2012 and "Tonight I'm Getting Over You" in February 2013. The album and its singles earned Carly Rae two Grammy Award nominations.

After spending much of 2012 opening for Justin Bieber's Believe Tour, Carly Rae was thrilled to get her own tour in summer 2013. When not headlining, the chart-topper took to the stage with pop star Kelly Clarkson, UK boy band The Wanted and Nashville pop-rock quartet Hot Chelle Rae.

Carly Rae was thrilled to record "Part of Your World" for Disney's *The Little Mermaid: Diamond Edition*, released in October 2013.

"I was actually in musical theater when I was in high school," she told HuffPost. "I played Little Orphan Annie, and Dorothy in *The Wizard of Oz* and Sandy in *Grease*. And I never thought I would get to bring musical theater back into my pop music career. So when they're like 'You get to be Ariel!' I was like, 'I get to? I get to be in a musical?' They're like, 'No, it's just one song.' And I'm like, 'I get to be in a musical!' So I totally skipped to the studio and let my theatrical side come out."

She says work on her next album began "the day *Kiss* was turned in." She's already written some songs that she thinks are keepers but says there's no real timetable for the project.

"I think *Kiss* was a bit of a rush," she told *Billboard* magazine in June 2013, "so I think I'll be kind of taking my time to make sure what I'm putting out there next feels like the strongest thing I can make."

Carly Rae plans to stay true to the sound that made her famous, but she hints that her new project will switch things up a bit. She told *Billboard*, it'll be "a pop album, but ... an album that is my own version of pop."

While others may fret about exactly what her version of pop looks like, and whether her next album will ensure her career longevity, Carly Rae says she's learned not to stress about the future.

"Usually, I take it a year at a time," she told *OK!* magazine in May 2013. "I do this thing where I have this bed sheet, and I pin it to the wall. I get markers and draw out this map of what's next, and what I have coming. It always ends up being completely different from my plans. I've learned, if anything, to expect the unexpected."

Carly Rae Jepsen performs during the 2013 Rays Summer Concert Series at Tropicana Field in St. Petersburg, Florida.

# CHAPTER SIX

# Bruno Mars

**B**runo Mars was just a toddler when he joined his family's musical act as an Elvis impersonator and quickly became one of the stars of the show. He continued to perform with his family throughout his childhood and eventually added an impersonation of Michael Jackson to his repertoire.

Bruno says performing songs by both The King of Rock and The Prince of Pop was a hands-on lesson in showmanship.

"The biggest thing is the command they both have on stage ... how they can control the crowd and the band," he told *the U-T San Diego* in June 2011. "I think there's a performance of Elvis on the Ed Sullivan (TV) show where he does 'Hound Dog.' At the end he slows it down, and — to me — it looked like an improv moment, not like something they rehearsed. It was like he (Presley) saw girls (in the audience) freaking out and said to himself: 'Watch me slow it down — and then really go nuts.' And he slows it down at the end and (then) starts

## ALL ACCESS

| | |
|---|---|
| **Full name:** | Peter Gene Hernandez |
| **Genre:** | Pop, reggae, R&B, funk, blues, rock |
| **First big hit:** | "Just the Way You Are," from the 2010 album *Doo-Wops & Hooligans*, was a 12-times-Platinum single that hit No. 1 in multiple countries and won Bruno a Grammy for Best Male Pop Vocal Performance. |
| **Label:** | Motown, Universal Motown, Atlantic, Elektra |
| **Website:** | www.brunomars.com |
| **On Twitter:** | @BrunoMars |
| **Twitter followers:** | 17.1 million |
| **Reputation:** | Well-coiffed Bruno often channels the Prince of Pop in his performances and has become a highly respected songwriter. |
| **Why we love him:** | His appeal is broad, with his concerts attracting cuddling couples, delirious dancers and families with young children. It's clear that his ability to blend and bend genres knows no bounds. |

his little dance, and he had them. The confidence Elvis and Michael exuded from stage, I'm a fan of."

Born Peter Gene Hernandez on October 8, 1985, in Honolulu, Hawaii, music was an integral part of Bruno's family life. His father, Pete, was a percussionist and his mother, Bernadette "Bernie," was a singer. His nickname came about when he was still an infant.

"The name Bruno came from baby times," his older sister, Jaime, told Oahu's *Midweek* newspaper in 2010. "Bruno was always so confident, independent, really strong-willed and kind of a brute – hence the name Bruno, and it kind of just stuck."

Even while performing with his family, Bruno and some pals formed a band called the School Boys that performed at Honolulu hotels. He was on stage most every day of every week.

When Bruno graduated from high school in 2002, he decided to move to Los Angeles to try to break into show business there. The process of auditioning and networking and not getting jobs was particularly frustrating for an artist who had already been working nonstop for more than a dozen years. He got signed to a label – Motown – but was released from his contract without ever putting out an album.

"That was a hard phone call to call my mom and dad and say, 'I'm no longer a signed artist and I've got to rethink this whole thing,'" he told *CBS Sunday Morning* in December 2012.

While some might have given up, Bruno started pawning his guitars to pay the bills and decided to redirect his creative energies; he needed to focus on songwriting.

"I only started writing songs when I moved up to L.A., because when I was in Hawaii, I never really needed to," he recalled. "But it stemmed from just learning that you have to do everything by yourself. It's not like what you see in movies, where you walk into a record company and you're given all these great songs to sing. You have to write the song the world is going to want to hear and play it over and over again."

Friends introduced Bruno to songwriter Philip Lawrence. The two joined with Ari Levine to form a songwriting/production team known as the Smeezingtons. The Smeezingtons have written or produced hits for artists including Flo Rida ("Right Round"), Travie McCoy ("Billionaire"), Brandy ("Long Distance"), Snoop Dogg & Wiz Khalifa ("Young Wild & Free") and Bad Meets Evil ("Lighters"). They also wrote K'Naan's "Wavin' Flag," which became the theme for the 2010 Winter Olympics.

After several years of working behind the scenes, Bruno worked his way back onstage when he was tapped to sing the chorus on B.o.B's 2010 song "Nothin' on You." The tune was a huge hit, climbing to No. 1 on the U.S. Billboard charts.

Within a few months, Bruno released his first solo single, "Just the Way You Are." The single preceded his debut album, *Doo-Wops & Hooligans*, which was released in October 2010. The album, which included hit singles "The Lazy Song" and "Grenade" peaked at No. 3 on the Billboard charts. The album, which has sold more than 6 million copies worldwide, was nominated for seven Grammy Awards, winning Best Pop Vocal Performance for "Just The Way You Are."

Bruno's second album, *Unorthodox Jukebox*, was released in December 2012 and peaked at No. 1 in the United States. The album sold more than 4 million copies during its first eight months of release. Hits from the album included "Locked Out of Heaven," "When I Was Your Man" and "Treasure."

In September 2013, the NFL announced that Bruno will be the featured performer during the Super Bowl XLVIII halftime show in February 2014. The honor put him in the same league as past half-time per-

formers including Madonna, Prince, the Rolling Stones, Paul McCartney, Beyonce, Michael Jackson and Justin Timberlake.

The chart-topping songs, sold-out shows, magazine covers, awards and, yes, the Super Bowl, are a welcome change for an artist who struggled for years to make it big.

"Ever since I was a kid, this is all I've wanted to do. I've wanted to do music.

"I've wanted to sing," he told *CBS Sunday Morning*. "All those hard times, if feels like it goes to show that if you put in the work and you don't stop believing, it can happen."

Yes, Bruno it can happen. And, thankfully it did.

Bruno Mars attends the 2013 MTV Video Music Awards in New York City.

Bruno Mars performs
during the 2013 Billboard
Music Awards at the MGM
Grand Garden Arena in
Las Vegas.

# CHAPTER SEVEN

# Ed Sheeran

As a lad learning to play the guitar back in Framlingham, Suffolk, England, Ed Sheeran dreamed of performing before crowds of screaming fans. He moved to London in 2008 to pursue those dreams but, even then, he couldn't have imagined the trajectory his career would take.

Ed released five independent EPs and performed in nearly any venue he could. He posted a video online that earned him an invitation to join mainstream British rapper Example on tour.

In 2010, with no gigs and no contacts, he traveled to Los Angeles. It was while he was playing an open-mic night that he caught the attention of singer-comedian Jamie Foxx. The Grammy winner was so impressed that he offered Ed the use of his recording studio and the run of his Hollywood home for the rest of his stay.

As 2010 wore on, the momentum continued to build. Thanks to YouTube, Ed's fan base was growing; among his most famous

# ALL ACCESS

| | |
|---|---|
| **Full name:** | Edward Christopher Sheeran |
| **Genre:** | Pop, rock, folk, rap, grime |
| **First big hit:** | "The A Team," the lead single from Ed's debut studio album entered the UK Singles Chart at No. 3 in June 2011, selling more than 58,000 copies in the first week. The song was released in the United States in late 2012 and peaked at No. 16. "The A Team" earned Ed his first Grammy nomination. |
| **Label:** | Asylum, Atlantic, Elektra |
| **Website:** | www.edsheeran.com |
| **On Twitter:** | @edsheeran |
| **Twitter followers:** | 8 million |
| **Reputation:** | He's a skilled singer and songwriter known as one of the nicest guys in the industry. The *Mail Online* said it best: *Sheeran is the folk star every kid would want their parents to like, and the rapper every parent would want their kids to listen to.* |
| **Why we love him:** | Oh, let us count the reasons: He's one of the hardest working artists in the business (in 2009, he played 312 gigs). His messy red hair, dozens of tattoos and sloppy black T-shirts ("Worst-Dressed Male in Britain" according to GQ) make him approachable. And, of course there's "The A Team," a song that's organically poetic and heart-meltingly lovely. |

fans were English footballer Rio Ferdinand and music superstar Elton John.

Finally, in early 2011, Ed signed a world-wide record deal with Asylum Records/Atlantic Records. His first commercially produced album, +, was released in September 2011. The CD, which contains the hit singles "The A Team" and "Lego House" was certified quintuple platinum in the United Kingdom. In 2012, he won two BRIT Awards for Best British Male and British Breakthrough. The album peaked at No. 5 on the U.S. Billboard 200 and earned him a Grammy nomination for Song of the Year for "The A Team."

Hundreds of thousands of U.S. music fans who still hadn't been exposed to Ed's music got a taste of it in 2013, when he spent six months touring with Taylor Swift. The red-headed musician, who co-wrote and recorded "Everything Has Changed" with Taylor, earned great reviews for his *Red Tour* performances:

*Opener Ed Sheeran continued his quest to charm the American masses, succeeding with an assured, confident set. He's already won over many souls with his mega-hit "The A-Team," but on Monday he further spread his message.*
*- The Los Angeles Times*

*Ed Sheeran had no elaborate props, no video projections or flying contraptions or stilt-walking dancers. But he worked the room with a single acoustic guitar, an amazingly powerful voice and a loop box that allowed him to construct enormous and at times cacophonous walls of sound. It was intense.*
*- Arizona Republic*

*Ed Sheeran was the highlight on the opening bill; his Pabst Theater show last fall was one of the year's most mesmerizing, where the easy-going singer-songwriter wielded a magical ability to bring a room filled with hundreds of screaming girls to a complete hush. Naturally, the Soldier Field set couldn't replicate such intimacy, but watching a guy alone on acoustic guitar captivate a stadium was an equally impressive sight.*
*- Milwaukee Journal Sentinel*

As if participating in one of the world's biggest concert tours wasn't enough, Ed's also been working on his next album, slated for release in February 2014. He says the follow-up will be different in theme from his debut.

"The first album I was inspired by everything around me," he told *The (London) Review* in September 2013. "I was kind of growing up surrounded by a lot of very interesting people and had a lot of stories." His new project, instead, promises to be inspired by his own relationship troubles.

"(For) this record, there has been more drama that has happened in my personal life," he said, "so I've written a lot about that."

Writing is something Ed does exceptionally well. He wrote or co-wrote 12 of the 13 tracks on + and co-wrote "Little Things" and "Over Again" with One Direction. Artist Direct calls him a songwriter "with the power to move anyone within earshot" and pal Taylor Swift says he's the "most in-demand songwriter in the world."

His status as a world-class musician was cemented when he was tapped to perform at Queen Elizabeth II's Diamond Jubilee, sang during the closing ceremonies of the 2012 Summer Olympics and performed a duet with Elton John at the 2013 Grammy Awards ceremony.

Yes, Ed has found success but the route there was not direct. Self-belief and perseverance got him through years of rejection and negativity.

"I felt every gig I played, fewer and fewer people would attend and this was going nowhere. Every single label I had gone to at the time had told me this song wasn't a hit, this song wouldn't work, and the fact that I was slightly chubby and ginger wasn't a good 'marketing tool' for them," he told *The (London) Independent* in July 2013.

"The way I maintained self-belief is that I knew I wasn't good at anything else so what else was I going to do, and secondly, with the whole look and songs that the labels rejected, I knew it was really important that I stay true to myself. Being an individual makes you stand out from the crowd."

When it comes to giving counsel to aspiring musicians, Ed has plenty to say. "I would say, you can never do enough gigs and you can never do enough songs. Make sure that every opportunity you can, play a show and every opportunity you can, write a song," he told *Interview* magazine in 2011.

"The more you write tunes, the better they will become. The more you do gigs, the better you will become. It's just kind of like the facts of life; the 'practice makes perfect' thing. Keep your fingers crossed, start from the bottom and work your way up."

Tried and true advice, for sure.

Ed Sheeran performs on NBC's *Today* show in July 2013.

# CHAPTER EIGHT

## Hunter Hayes

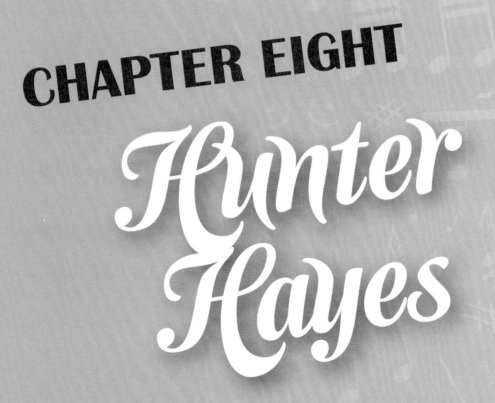

Hunter Hayes has accomplished things most musicians only dream of:

- Singing and playing the accordion with Hank Williams Jr. in front of 200,000 people at the age of four.
- Entertaining President Bill Clinton at a White House party.
- Being inducted into the Louisiana Music Hall of Fame as a 21-year-old.

Yes, Hunter is one lucky guy. But he's also talented too – not to mention one of the hardest working musicians in the business.

Hunter was born September 9, 1991, in Breaux Bridge, a town of 8,100 people in south-central Louisiana. His parents, Leo, manager of a boat supply store, and Lynette Hayes, a school teacher, say that Hunter was drawn to music from birth. When his grandmother gave him a toy accordion for his second birthday, he immediately began playing Cajun songs he'd heard on the radio. This wasn't just noise, it was music – being played well and from the heart.

# ALL ACCESS

**Full name:** Hunter Easton Hayes

**Genre:** Country, cajun

**First big hit:** "Wanted," released to radio on March 5, 2012, became Hunter's first No. 1 single and made him the youngest solo male act to top Hot Country Songs. The song was nominated for a 2013 Grammy Award for Best Country Solo Performance.

**Label:** Atlantic

**Website:** www.hunterhayes.com

**On Twitter:** @HunterHayes

**Twitter followers:** 850,000

**Reputation:** When it comes to music, Hunter has a laser-like focus – no hobbies, no days off. "With me, it's always going to be music," he says in his website bio. "That's the one thing I know. That is my thing. That is my place. I make music because it's the only way I can breathe. This is how I want to spend the rest of my life."

**Why we love him:** He's been performing since he was a toddler and writes his own music – often inspired by real-life experiences. If you're into overachievers, Hunter's your guy. He wrote or co-wrote every track on his debut self-titled CD, played every instrument and performed his own background vocals. Bam!

By the time he was five, Hunter was regularly playing with Cajun bands at a neighborhood restaurant called Mulatte's and had graduated to a custom-made accordion designed especially for his small hands. The tiny blonde prodigy became a regional celebrity, earning guest spots on local TV shows and even landing a small part in the 1997 film *The Apostle* with Robert Duvall. The Academy Award winner was so taken with Hunter that he gave the boy a guitar for his sixth birthday. "I thought that was the coolest thing in the world," Hunter told *Parade* magazine in August 2013.

As with the accordion, Hunter taught himself to play the guitar – and the bass guitar and piano and drums. "I've never had the patience to sit down and learn from anyone," he said. "So with the guitar, and with every subsequent instrument and piece of studio equipment, it's been a process of experimentation – pressing every button I can."

While classmates were busy mastering the alphabet and simple addition, Hunter began writing music. His songwriting and performing continued into his teen years, when he began recording and producing his own music. His compositions have been influenced by a diverse group of artists, from Garth Brooks and the Beatles to Michael Buble.

"At school, I was a quiet kid. I was really shy," he said on his official website. "My safe zone was music. In writing music, I had my friend, the one thing that would never let me down. Writing songs was like me keeping a journal. I really took it seriously when I realized how powerful of a tool it was and how much I needed it."

Hunter built a small studio in his house and skipped out on school activities and parties so he could spend his time there, making music.

By the time he was in high school, his parents began taking him to Nashville, where he met music industry insiders who mentored Hunter. In 2008, the whole Hayes family moved to Nashville and Hunter signed on with Universal Music Publishing Group as a songwriter. Two years later, he co-wrote "Play" for Rascal Flatts' album *Nothing Like This*. In September 2010, he signed with Atlantic Records Nashville.

Hunter, who had previously released five independent albums, finally began work on his first commercial project. He asked Atlantic Records to take a chance on him and let him play all the instruments on his debut album. It was something he'd done on his 2008 project *Songs About Nothing*, so he knew it could be done. He says it took producer Dann Huff a while to warm up to the idea.

"But to his credit, and to everyone's credit, everybody was open-minded, positive about it, and optimistic," he said. "I think everybody's mindset was, 'Why not try it? Let's see if it works.'"

Not only does Hunter play every instrument on his self-titled debut – there are 30 in all – he also wrote or co-wrote every track and sings every vocal track, with the exception of the CD's encore tracks.

The album's debut single, "Storm Warning," was released in May 2011; it peaked at No. 14. When his second single, "Wanted" climbed to No. 1 on the country charts in September

2012, Hunter made history as the youngest solo male act to top the radio tally; he was 21 years and two weeks of age, surpassing a record set in 1973 by Johnny Rodriguez, who was 21 years, three months and three weeks old when his song "You Always Come Back to Hurting Me" took top honors.

*Hunter Hayes* was released on October 11, 2011. The CD's third and fourth singles, "Somebody's Heartbreak" and "I Want Crazy" peaked at No. 1 and No. 2 on the Country Airplay chart respectively.

The young artist, who has toured with Rascal Flatts, Taylor Swift, Carrie Underwood and headlined his own Most Wanted Tour, has been named by Martin Guitars as its latest brand ambassador. He's been racking up music awards, including the Country Music Association's New Artist of the Year (2012), Teen Choice Awards for top Male Country Artist (2012 and 2013) and CMT's Nationwide Insurance On Your Side Award for best new live act (2013). He was also nominated for three Grammys – for Best New Artist, Best Country Solo Performance and Best Country Album at the 2013 Grammy Awards.

No matter how many red carpets he walks or concerts he sells out, Hunter says he still has his share of "OMG" moments.

"Meeting Stevie Wonder was a massive, lifetime achievement for me," he told *Parade*. "He's one of the sweetest people. I sense a kindred spirit in him, and I hope he'd say the same. Actually, he did. He said, 'What I feel from you is you live, breathe, eat, sleep, drink music, and I can relate to that.' It was really cool to share that with him and to feel that there's somebody else who always wants to make noise."

Noise? If that's what you call it, Hunter, please keep making it!

Hunter Hayes performs during the 2013 CMA Music Festival in Nashville.

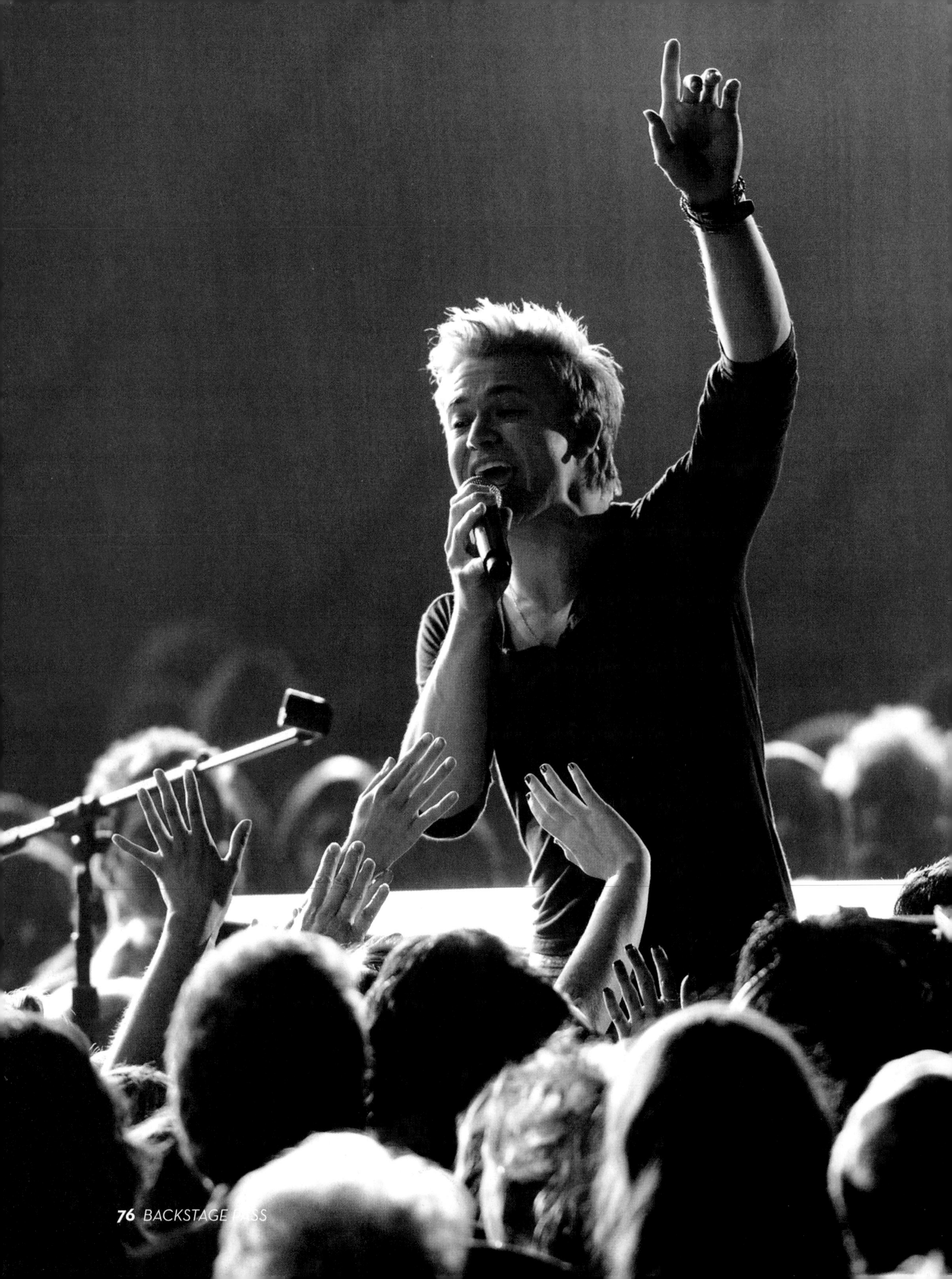

Hunter Hayes rehearses at Nashville's Bridgestone Arena in preparation for the 2013 CMT Music Awards.

# CHAPTER NINE

# One Direction

Every time a One Direction song plays on the radio, fans breathe a collective sigh of relief. They know that the band they love came together purely by chance. These guys weren't childhood buddies or music school classmates.

These five guys – total strangers – auditioned for 2010's *The X Factor* as individuals. They made it through preliminary rounds but were cut at the boot camp stage of the competition.

Then – SURPRISE! – four girls along with Harry Styles, Liam Payne, Louis Tomlinson, Niall Horan, and Zayn Malik were called back onto the stage.

Judges Simon Cowell, Louis Walsh, and Nichole Scherzinger were willing to give these nine performers a second chance. The guys would perform together and the

# ALL ACCESS

**Full name:** One Direction consists of Niall James Horan, Zayn Jawaad Malik, Liam James Payne, Harry Edward Styles, and Louis William Tomlinson

**Genre:** Pop, rock

**First big hit:** "What Makes You Beautiful" was the lead single from 1D's debut studio album, *Up All Night*. The song debuted at No. 1 on the UK, Irish and Scottish Singles Charts and reached the Top 10 in Australia, New Zealand, Canada and Japan. It peaked at No. 4 on the U.S. Billboard Hot 100. With more than 5 million copies sold worldwide, the track is the best-selling song by a boy band in digital history and is among the best-selling singles of all time.

**Label:** Syco, Columbia

**Website:** www.onedirectionmusic.com

**On Twitter:** @onedirection

**Twitter followers:** 15.8 million follow their official band Twitter. Each of the guys has his own very active Twitter account; collectively, the five of them have 70 million followers.

**Reputation:** One Direction was first known as the band that was brought together as part of the British TV singing competition *The X Factor*. The guys have since cemented their reputation as charming heartthrobs who can actually sing.

**Why we love them:** Their songs are undeniably catchy (you know you sing along every time you hear "What Makes You Beautiful" or "Up All Night.") The guys are handsome, well-dressed and goofy. Plus, those accents are beyond adorable!

Liam Payne was born and raised in Wolverhampton, England. He also auditioned for *X Factor* in 2008 but was sent home early in the competition.

Louis Tomlinson, a native of Doncaster, South Yorkshire, England, is known as the group's biggest prankster. He is always cracking jokes and making fans laugh, especially in 1D's video diaries.

Niall Horan is One Direction's only Irish member. Family members say he had a flair for entertainment, even as a youngster. Though, his cousin Robert Horan, told the *London Mail:* 'I always thought he'd end up being a comedian.'

girls would perform together, and they could continue to compete as groups. Were they interested? Yes, of course they were.

Just one misstep – one poorly performed song or super cranky judge – and One Direction might never have happened. And, while chance brought them together, it's clear talent has kept them on top.

These handsome young men, who ended up winning third place on the TV talent show, are selling albums and concert tickets at breakneck speed and melting the hearts of girls and young women around the globe.

When the band's debut CD, *Up All Night*, was released in March 2012, One Direction became the first UK group ever to debut at No. 1 on the U.S. Billboard 200 album chart. The feat earned the guys a spot in the *Guinness Book of World Records*.

In a statement released by the group's record label, Niall noted: "When we got put together as a group, we couldn't imagine ourselves coming to America, let alone releasing our album here, so for us to be sitting at the top of the U.S. album charts is unbelievable."

Within the first week of its release, One Direction sold more than 176,000 copies of its debut album, *Up All Night*. The CD shot straight to the top of the digital charts within minutes of its official release on March 13, 2012. When the group made its American television debut in March 2012, a crowd of more than 10,000 screaming fans showed outside the *Today* show studios at New York City's Rockefeller Center, prompting NBC to hire additional security.

"The *Today* show for me was the most

amazing thing," Liam told The *Washington Post*. "There wasn't enough room for everybody to come up. They couldn't even see us. They were just hanging around to get a glimpse of what's going on."

Young fans already knew these guys were the real deal and their reaction made the rest of America sit up and take notice. *Up All Night* became the first album by a boy band to sell 500,000 digital copies in the United States.

In December 2011, One Direction embarked on its first headlining concert tour. The *Up All Night* Tour sold out shows in the United Kingdom, Australia and North America. A recording of a concert from the tour, *Up All Night: The Live Tour*, was released in May 2012; more than one million copies of the DVD have been sold globally.

One Direction's second studio album, *Take Me Home*, was released in November 2012. Its lead single, "Live While We're Young," was released in September 2012 and reached the Top 10 in almost every country it charted in. The album and its second single, "Little Things," simultaneously debuted at No. 1 in the United Kingdom, making One Direction the youngest act in British chart history to top both the singles and album charts.

In the United States, *Take Me Home* sold 540,000 copies in its first week of release and debuted atop the Billboard 200.

According to the IFPI (International Federation of the Phonographic Industry), *Up All Night* and *Take Me Home* were the No. 3 and No. 4 best-selling albums of 2012 globally, selling 4.5 million and 4.4 million units respectively.

One Direction's second concert tour, the *Take Me Home* Tour, launched in February 2013, with more than 100 shows in Europe, North America, and Australia.

The band released "Best Song Ever," the lead single from its third album, in July 2013. The album, *Midnight Memories*, was released in November 2013 and is more rock-oriented than the group's first two projects

"It is a much better album this time round and this personally (is) our favorite of the three albums and we're just really excited," Niall Horan told the U.K.'s 95-106 Capital FM. "It's very edgy, loads of guitars, loads of drums and then obviously you've got your ballads there too."

One Direction's 3D movie, *This Is Us*, was released in August 2013 and its first stadium tour, Where We Are, is set to begin in April 2014. In all, the guys are the faces of a business empire worth nearly $1 billion, with sales of records, DVDs, concert tickets and licensing deals that include everything from lunchboxes and T-shirts to décor and fragrances.

These well-coiffed young men are five of the most recognizable individuals in the free world. Fans camp out to catch glimpses of them as they walk into TV studios or stadiums, pandemonium breaks out when a fan tweets information – true or not – about which hotel they're staying at. Chaos is their new normal.

"I don't think you can ever get used to being this famous," Harry Styles told GQ magazine in September 2013. "I've learnt how to keep things separate or at a distance. I've nothing to hide. But seeing this as work, like a job, means I can take a step back. It's me right now in front of you and in the papers, but it's not all of me. If you give yourself entirely to the business, you'd end up going mad. And I'm not mad. Not yet."

No, Harry, you're not mad. And for that, your fans are very, very glad.

Niall Horan, Louis Tomlinson, Liam Payne, Zayn Malik, and Harry Styles of One Direction attend the 2013 MTV Video Music Awards in New York City.

Before becoming famous, Harry Styles worked in a bakery in his hometown of Holmes Chapel, Cheshire, England. Handsome Harry is now known as the band's "ladies man."

Zayn Malik grew up in West Lane Baildon, Bradford, England. In addition to being a great musician, Zayn is also a visual artist. He's credited for creating some of the illustrations on One Direction's debut CD cover.

# CHAPTER TEN

Justin Bieber

These days, every pop star wannabe is trying to get discovered on YouTube. Today, it seems a logical path to fame. When Justin Bieber did it back in 2008 – just three years after the video-sharing website was created – he was a pioneer.

Justin was 12 years old when he started posting homemade videos of himself performing. There were videos of him rapping Lil Bow Wow's "Basketball" and one in which he's wearing a tie and dress shirt singing Ne-Yo's "So Sick." He's caught on tape in his bathroom singing "Back at One" by Brian McKnight and he sits on the sofa in another, strumming the guitar and singing Justin Timberlake's "Cry Me a River."

Justin's videos caught the attention of web-browsing tweens. They emailed links of the videos to friends, who sent them to friends and soon, Justin's YouTube videos went viral.

Of course, it wasn't just 12-year-old girls who were enjoying Justin's sweet voice.

## ALL ACCESS

| | |
|---|---|
| **Full name:** | Justin Drew Bieber |
| **Genre:** | Pop, rock, R&B |
| **First big hit:** | "Baby," the lead single from Justin's debut album, was released in January 2010 and became an international hit. It charted at No. 5 on the U.S. Billboard Hot 100 and reached the Top 10 in several international markets. As of mid-2013, it is the best-selling song in U.S. history. |
| **Label:** | Island, Teen Island, RBMG, School Boy |
| **Website:** | www.justinbiebermusic.com |
| **On Twitter:** | @justinbieber |
| **Twitter followers:** | 46 million |
| **Reputation:** | Justin is the face of a new generation of performers whose careers were launched thanks to videos they posted on YouTube. Since hitting it big, he's become known as a consummate performer with smooth vocals and really cool dance moves. |
| **Why we love him:** | Bieber Fever is hard to shake. No matter how many times JB has his monkey seized in a German airport or how often he scuffles with the paparazzi, we will insist that he's simply misunderstood. He's still a kid and he's dealing with some very stressful situations. Besides, he's a talented vocalist and a supreme showman. |

Music promoter Scooter Braun was up late one night, researching another singer on his computer. That's when he stumbled across a home video of Justin singing Aretha Franklin's "Respect."

"It was such raw talent, my gut just went wild," he told *Time* magazine.

Braun was so impressed that he vowed to track down the Canadian kid with the big voice and baby face. He searched through photo archives to find the theatre where Justin had been videotaped performing. He phoned Justin's school principal and board members and begged them to put him in touch with Justin's mother.

At first, Braun's intensity frightened Justin's parents, Pattie Mallette and Jeremy Bieber. It took some convincing and even a prayer session with church leaders, but ultimately they decided to take the meeting.

Braun flew Justin and his mother from their home in Stratford, Ontario, Canada to Atlanta – their first flight ever. It was during that trip to Atlanta that Justin bumped into his idol, Usher, in the music studio parking lot. Justin eagerly offered to sing for Usher, who politely refused.

Justin was disappointed but not discouraged. He and his mom talked strategy with Braun. They made plans about the best ways to build a fan base, which labels to approach, and which songs best suited his vocal style.

For six months, they posted new videos on YouTube. Justin personally responded to fans who posted comments. He used fans' names and talked to them like long-lost friends. He was approachable. He was ac-cessible. He was handsome and talented. He was everything Braun thought he needed to be – except for one thing.

Record label executives weren't willing to gamble on an unknown teenage singer.

"They kept telling me, 'He's not backed by Disney. He doesn't have a TV show. He's a nobody,'" Braun told *Time*.

While industry executives weren't yet biting, news of Justin's talent was quickly spreading among other artists. Usher saw the videos and called to ask for a meeting with Justin. Braun's reply? "Get in line."

"Scooter (Braun) said, 'Justin is interested in this kid,'" Usher told the *New York Times*. "I said, 'Justin? You mean Justin Timberlake?'"

Yes, the six-time Grammy winner was flying JB to Los Angeles to talk about possible music deals.

Usher, not wanting to miss out on what could be the next-big-thing, jumped into action. He rearranged his schedule so he could meet with Justin first. He was not about to lose a bidding war with Timberlake.

Eventually, Usher won out and became part of the team that would propel Justin from small town Canadian unknown to global superstar.

Since that first flight to Atlanta in 2008, Justin has made music history:

He's the first solo artist to have four singles enter the Top 40 before releasing his debut album. He is also the first artist ever to have seven songs from a debut album chart on the Billboard Hot 100.

Five of his nine album releases have climbed to No. 1 on the Billboard charts: *Believe, My World 2.0, My Worlds, Never*

*Say Never – The Remixes* and *Under the Mistletoe.*

His single "Baby" spent a remarkable 317 weeks on the Billboard charts.

His 2010 autobiography, *Justin Bieber: First Step 2 Forever*, was on the New York Times children's bestseller list for 18 consecutive weeks.

He's a social media mogul. His official You-Tube channel has 6.4 million subscribers. In the Twitter-sphere, he has 46 million followers. And, on Facebook, the artist is "liked" by more than 57.2 million users.

His 2011 concert documentary, *Justin Bieber: Never Say Never*, grossed $98.4 million worldwide. The film bumped Michael Jackson's *This Is It* from the top rung to become the most successful concert-themed movie at the domestic box office.

Of course, not everything about Justin's life is sparkly and wonderful. In recent months, he's been the subject of some not-so-flattering media coverage. He's endured a very public breakup with singer Selena Gomez, has had repeated run-ins with the paparazzi, was criticized for starting concerts up to 90 minutes late, and has been charged with reckless driving.

Usher says Justin is like any other young person – except that, thanks to social media, he's being forced to make his mistakes in the spotlight.

"I don't look at it as a negative," he said during a May 2013 appearance on *Ellen*. I look at it as (being) a teenager. He's a teenager having to live his life in front of a camera. Imagine if you had to do that as a teenager."

Justin's 154-show *Believe* Tour wraps up in late 2013. The young singer has said he may take a break from music after that – or not. He's leaked pictures of himself working on his next studio project and rapper Future has been front and center in those photos.

Rap, pop, rock? Beliebers don't seem to care – as long as Justin keeps making music.

Justin Bieber performs during the 2013 Billboard Music Awards at the MGM Grand Garden Arena in Las Vegas.

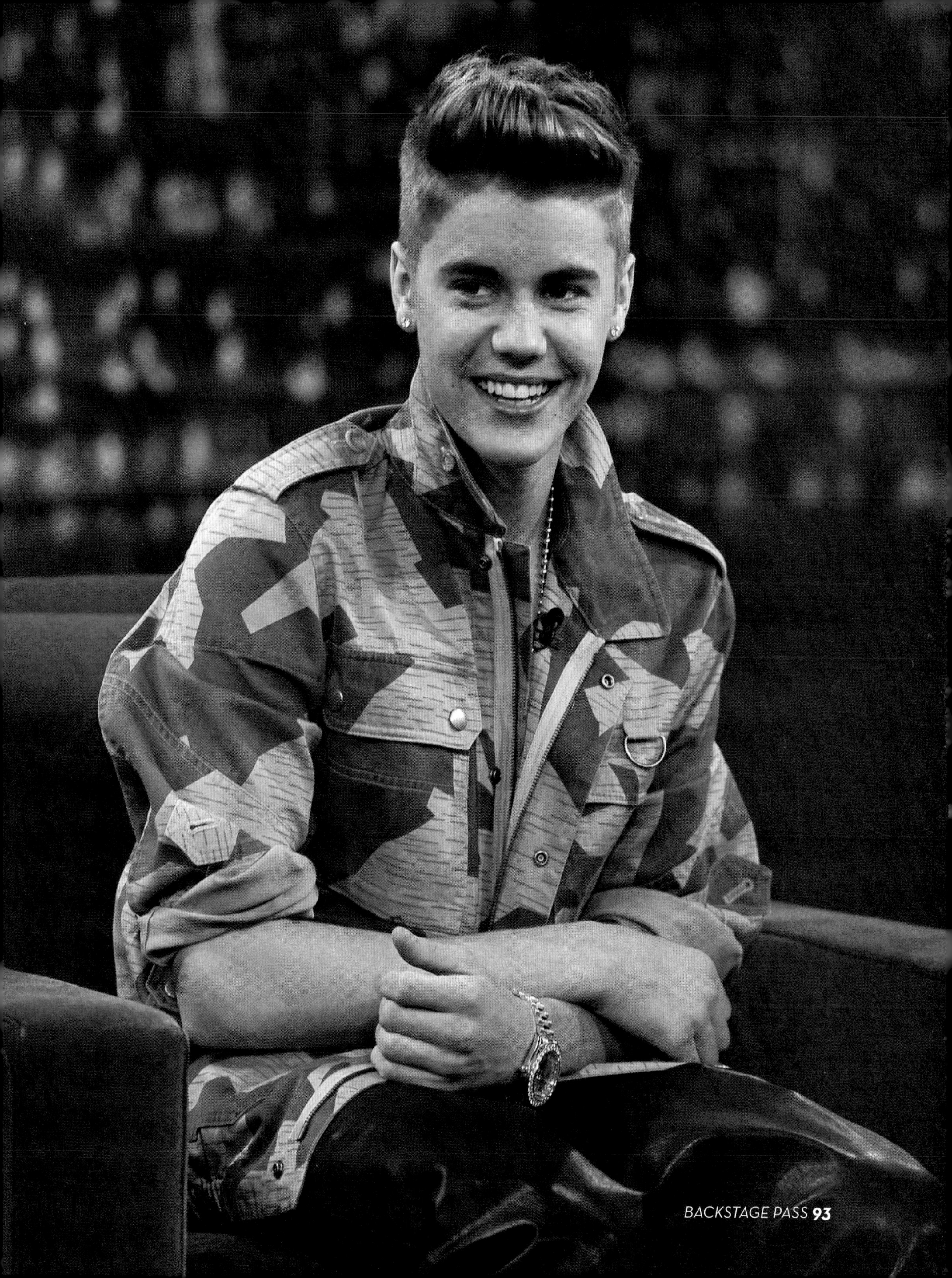

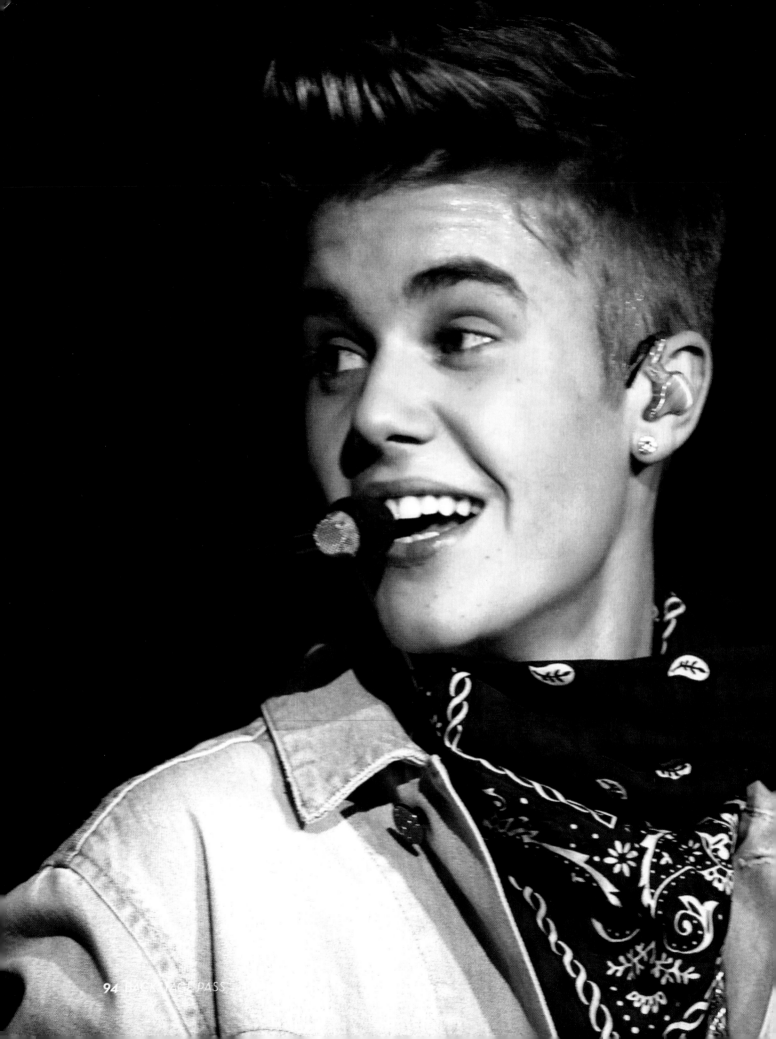

Justin Bieber wows a New York City crowd in August 2013 as part of his Believe Tour.

Singapore fans got to hear their musical idol when Justin Bieber performed at a Formula One Grand Prix event there in September 2013.